AF206989

GREEN ANACONDA

WORLD'S COOLEST SNAKES

BRITTANY CANASI

rourkeeducationalmedia.com

Fast Facts

WORLD'S COOLEST SNAKES

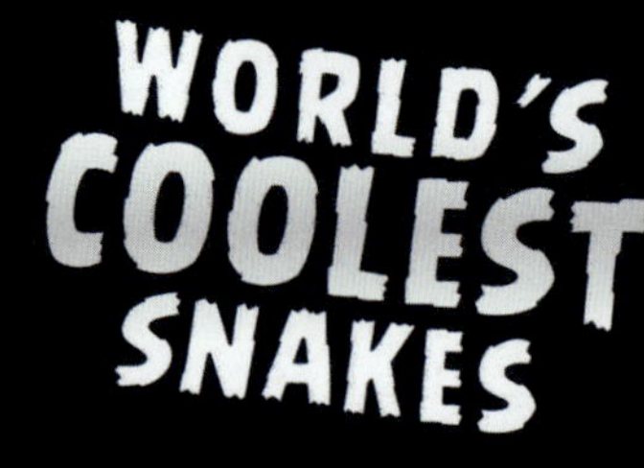

Family: Boidae

Genus: *Eunectes*

Number of species: 1

Species: *Eunectes murinus*

Diet: pigs, deer, birds, jaguars, large rodents, and other reptiles

Range: All over South America, Trinidad

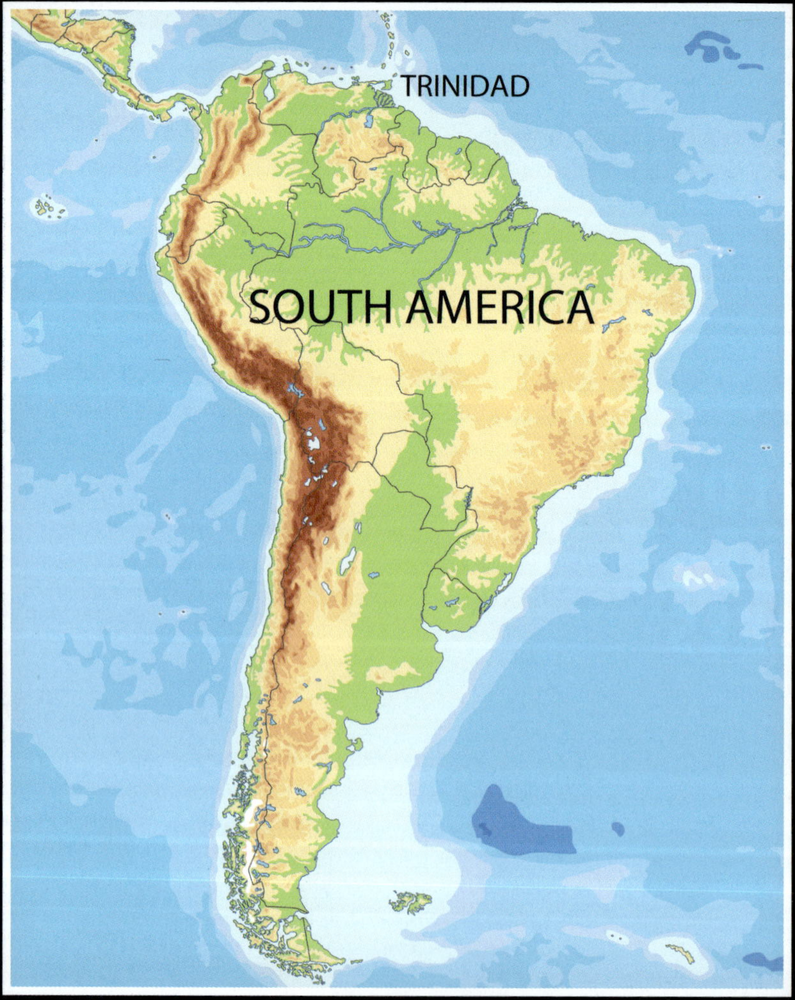

Table of Contents

Sizing Up

Green anacondas are the heaviest snakes in the world. They can weigh up to 550 pounds (249.5 kilograms). That's as much as two baby elephants combined!

The green anaconda is a member of the boa family. Like other boas, this snake isn't poisonous. It kills its prey by **constricting**. One of its nicknames is "the water boa."

Fact or Fiction?

Male green anacondas are larger than females.

FICTION! The average female is 15.1 feet long (4.6 meters). The average male is 9.8 feet long (3 meters).

It's All Relative
There are more than 40 species of boas. That's a big family!

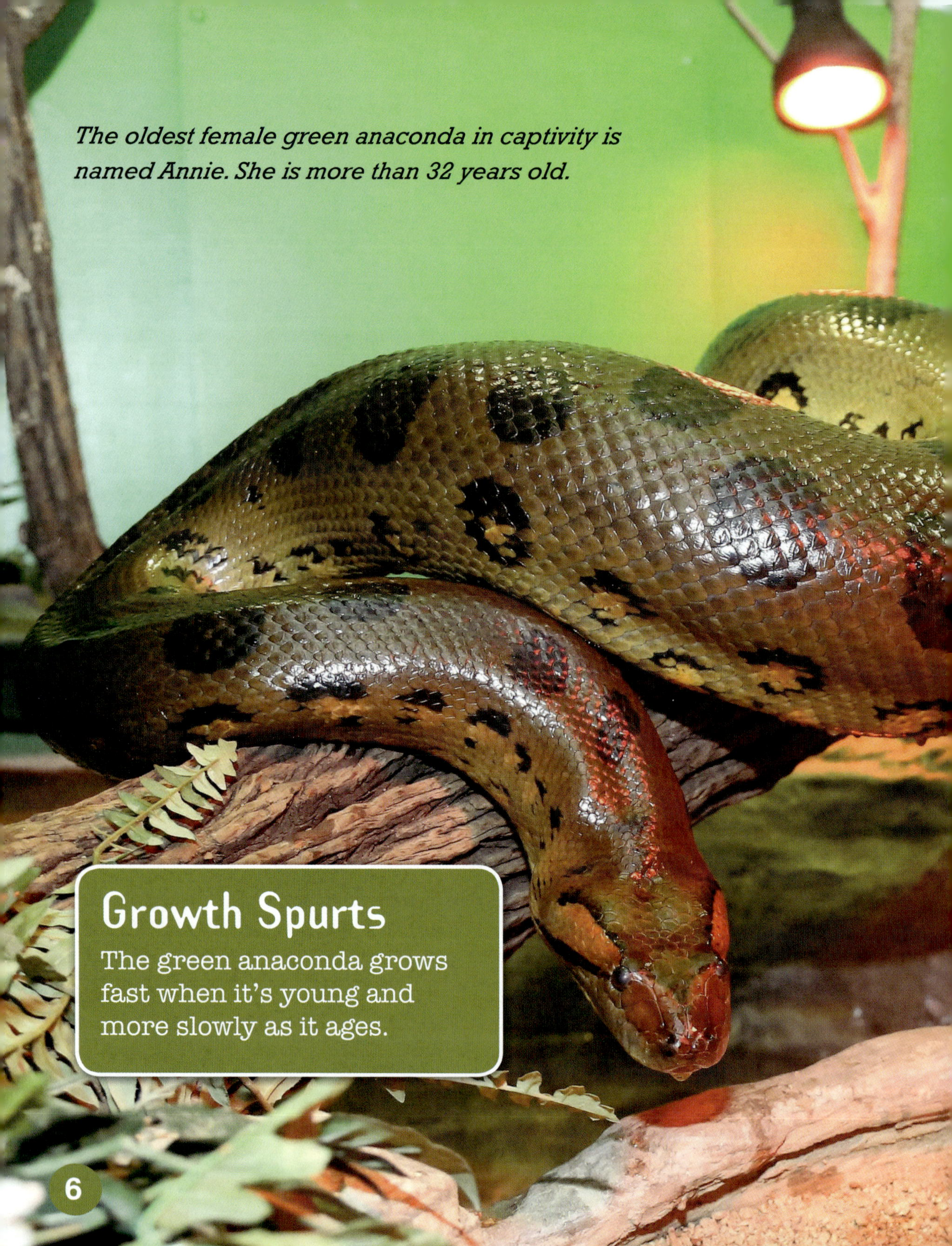

Growth Spurts

The green anaconda grows fast when it's young and more slowly as it ages.

Green anacondas live about ten years in the wild. They can live about 30 years in **captivity**. Like all snakes, they never really stop growing, and their bodies can grow more than twelve inches (30.5 centimeters) in **diameter**.

Anacondas live in swamps, **marshlands**, and rainforests. They're mostly found in South America and Trinidad.

Because of their size, they don't move fast on land. They spend a lot of time in the water, where they can move quickly and silently. If they want some sun, you might find them resting on a branch above the water. And when they're ready to get wet, they drop back in!

Fact or Fiction?

The scales underneath a green anaconda's tail are like a human fingerprint.

FACT! Every human fingerprint is unique, just like the scales under every green anaconda's tail.

Green anacondas, like humans, are apex predators. This means they are at the top of their food chain.

The green anaconda spends more time underwater than any member of the boa family. Their genus name, Eunectes, means "good swimmer" in Greek.

Their eye and nasal openings are both on top of their head, like on an alligator. This allows them to stay **submerged** while they wait for prey. They can stay underwater for up to 10 minutes.

Lies about Size

Green anacondas have been reported to be as big as 50 feet (15.2 meters) or longer. But claims like these can't be trusted because they haven't been proven for several reasons:

1. A person's claim must be verified by an official source, such as a museum or a scientist.

2. It can be hard to trap and transport the anaconda from its habitat to an official shortly after its death.

3. If just the skin is transported, the skin could have been stretched to twice its original size through the **tanning** process.

There could be longer anacondas than what's been verified (especially in remote parts of the rainforest), but no one's been able to provide proof.

Green anacondas, like all species of anaconda, prefer to live alone. They have their own territories that can cover an area up to a quarter of a square mile (0.65 square kilometers). Anacondas will usually stay out of others' territories.

During dry season, the green anaconda may find water somewhere else, or bury itself in mud and become dormant. This means they stop hunting and only come out when the dry season ends.

A Big Feast

As a member of the boa family, the green anaconda uses the muscles in its body to wrap around prey and cut off their circulation, or blood supply. They can also grab their prey and drag it underwater until the prey drowns.

When a green anaconda hunts, it grabs hold of its prey with its sharp teeth. While its mouth is holding the prey steady, the snake will wrap around and constrict the prey until it dies. And green anacondas don't chew—they swallow their prey whole! They'll unhinge their jaw to expand their mouth if the prey is large.

Anacondas eat a variety of animals, including pigs, deer, birds, jaguars, large rodents, and other reptiles. Their skin stretches, and they don't have a **sternum**, so their body can expand when they eat large prey.

Fact or Fiction?

The green anaconda is a night owl.

FACT! The green anaconda is **nocturnal**, so it hunts primarily at night.

They can go weeks in between meals, even months if their last meal was big enough. Larger meals are rarer, though, because it's easier to catch smaller meals.

Caimans are predators of other species of anaconda (like the yellow anaconda), but they are prey to the green anaconda.

Mother of Giants

Green anacondas take a break from being anti-social during mating season. The female releases chemicals that attract males, and several males travel to her. Mating season lasts between March and May.

Female green anacondas pick their mate from a breeding ball. A breeding ball has up to 12 male snakes that wrestle to compete for the female. Breeding balls can last for weeks.

A Bed of Anacondas
A group of anacondas is called a bed or a knot.

A female green anaconda is **pregnant** for six to seven months, and she does not eat during this time. This could be because hunting could harm the babies. But once the baby snakes are born, they're on their own. Green anaconda moms do not care for their young.

A Big Family

The size of a green anaconda's litter depends on the size of the mother. The average litter size is two or three dozen.

A female green anaconda can have a litter of up to 50 snakes at a time! When baby anacondas are born, they are about two feet (61 centimeters) long. They can swim and hunt not long after birth. They are full-grown by the time they are four years old.

Giant Slayers

The green anaconda does not have many predators. Sometimes a jaguar can kill an anaconda, but it's usually out of self-defense.

Most predators are only dangerous to anacondas when they are babies or old and weak. For instance, a group of piranhas will gang up on an old anaconda.

piranhas

Komodo dragon

A Giant Runner-Up

The green anaconda is the heaviest scaled reptile in the world. A distant second is the Komodo dragon.

Humans are the green
anaconda's biggest predator.
Deforestation, land development,
and hunting are the anaconda's
biggest killers.

Locals will sometimes kill green
anacondas on sight out of fear. They
worry that the snake could attack
a human or one of their livestock.
While the green anaconda could eat
a pig, they rarely attack people.

Can Anacondas Eat Humans?

Anacondas have been called "man-eaters"
in legends for a very long time. This legend
has even inspired movies where anacondas
hunt humans. There have been reports of
anacondas eating people, but none of these
have been verified. However, scientists do
think an anaconda could eat a person, since
their typical prey are stronger and faster
than humans.

The Huaorani, Waorani or Waodani, also known as the Waos, believe it is an act of bravery to catch and release green anaconda.

Colossal Cage

The green anaconda can be kept in captivity, but only by experienced caretakers. These large snakes can be aggressive.

Green anacondas need a humid environment, similar to a rainforest. The cages of captive anacondas must have an area for heat and an area with shade.

Nightmare Neighbor

Green anacondas are now found in other parts of the world where they don't belong. These places have similar climates, like the Florida Everglades. The green anaconda shows up in the wild either from being smuggled into the country or being abandoned as pets.

Both green anacondas and Burmese pythons have become invasive species in parts of Florida.

In these new places, they have no natural predators, and they disrupt the ecosystem. The green anaconda becomes an invasive species. Invasive species are dangerous because scientists cannot tell what damage is done until it's too late. An invasive species can cause a **native** species to go extinct.

Invasive species disrupt the ecosystem by eating other animals' prey. The green anaconda eats a lot of the same animals an alligator would.

Glossary

captivity (kap-TIV-i-tee): held or trapped by people

constricting (kuhn-STRIKT-ing): slowing or stopping a natural flow by making a passage narrower; to squeeze

deforestation (dee-fohr-eh-STAY-shun): clearing a wide area of trees

diameter (dye-AM-it-ur): the length of a straight line through the center of a circle

marshlands (MAHRSH-lands): areas consisting of low-lying, waterlogged land

native (NAY-tiv): a person who was born in or lives in a particular country or place

nocturnal (nahk-TUR-nuhl): happening at night

pregnant (PREG-nuhnt): having a baby or young growing inside the uterus

sternum (STUR-nuhm): bone or cartilage that connects the ribs

submerged (suhb-MURJD): sunk or plunged beneath the surface of a liquid, especially water

tanning (TAN-neeng): to make animal skin into leather by soaking it in a chemical solution

Index

Show What You Know

1. Why is it hard to verify a green anaconda's size?

2. How many snakes are in a typical green anaconda litter?

3. What does the location of their nasal and eye openings let them do?

4. What does the green anaconda eat?

5. Where does it hunt best?

Further Reading

Avery, Sebastian, *Snakes on the Hunt: Anacondas*, Rosen Publishing, 2017.

Mattison, Chris, *Snake*, Dorling Kindersley, 2016.

Buckley Jr., James, *Snakes!*, Animal Planet, 2017.

About the Author

Brittany Canasi's job is in cartoons, and her passion is in writing. She has a B.A. in Creative Writing from Florida State University. If she could be any snake, it would be the flying tree snake, because it sounds like a better way to travel than driving. She lives in Los Angeles with her husband and very scruffy dogs.

www.rourkeeducationalmedia.com

PHOTO CREDITS: Cover ©Matthijs Kuijpers/Alamy Stock Photo, Pg 1 © By wayak, Pg 2 © MappingTechOne Copyright.2017. Cartarium., Pg 5 ©mauritius images GmbH/Alamy Stock Photo, Pg 6 ©Xinhua/Alamy Stock Photo, Pg 9 ©By Marcelina Zygula, Pg 10 ©WaterFrame/Alamy Stock Photo, Pg 11 ©Wrangel|Dreamstime.com, Pg 13 ©All Canada Photos/Alamy Stock Photo, Pg 15 ©Bernard Bialorucki/Alamy Stock Photo, Pg 16 ©Tony Crocetta/Biosphoto/Minden Pictures, Pg 19 ©Francois Savigny/Biosphoto/Minden Pictures, Pg 20 ©By LABETAA Andre, Pg 21 ©By Patrick K. Campbel, Pg 22 ©MikeLane45, Pg 23 ©Elenmay, guenterguni, Pg 25 ©BNX6AK, Pg 26 ©By Gabor Kovacs Photography, Pg 27 ©AX8BM7, Pg 28 ©FWC, Pg 29 ©THEPALMER

Edited by: Keli Sipperley
Cover by: Kathy Walsh
Interior design by: Rhea Magaro-Wallace

Library of Congress PCN Data

Green Anaconda / Brittany Canasi
 (World's Coolest Snakes)
 ISBN 978-1-64156-486-1 (hard cover)
 ISBN 978-1-64156-612-4 (soft cover)
 ISBN 978-1-64156-725-1 (e-Book)
Library of Congress Control Number: 2018930705

Rourke Educational Media
Printed in the United States of America,
North Mankato, Minnesota